PHILIPPINES

MAJOR WORLD NATIONS
PHILIPPINES

Jessie Wee

CHELSEA HOUSE PUBLISHERS
Philadelphia

Chelsea House Publishers

Copyright © 1999 by Chelsea House Publishers,
a division of Main Line Book Co.
All rights reserved.
Printed in Hong Kong

First Printing.

1 3 5 7 9 8 6 4 2

Library of Congress Cataloging-in-Publication Data

Wee, Jessie.
The Philippines / Jessie Wee.
p. cm. — (Major world nations)
Includes index.
Summary: Explores the people, history, culture, land, climate, and
economy of the Philippines, the only Christian nation in Asia.
ISBN 0-7910-4984-1(hc)
1. Philippines—Juvenile literature. [1. Philippines.] I. Title.
II. Series.
DS655.W44 1998
959.9—dc21   98-4314
CIP
AC

ACKNOWLEDGEMENTS

The Author and Publishers are grateful to the following organizations for permission to
reproduce copyright material in this book and for assistance given in its preparation:
Andes Press Agency; Hutchison Library; Mansell Collection; the Philippine Ministry of
Tourism, Singapore, and the Philippine Tourist Board, London.

CONTENTS

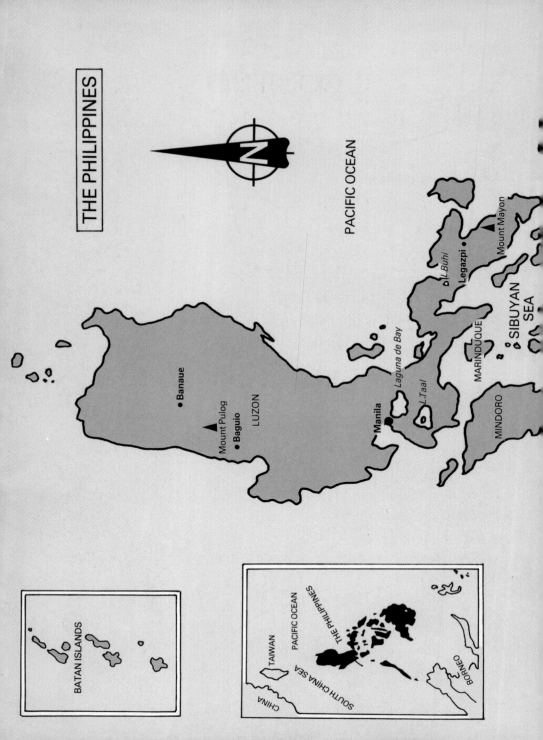

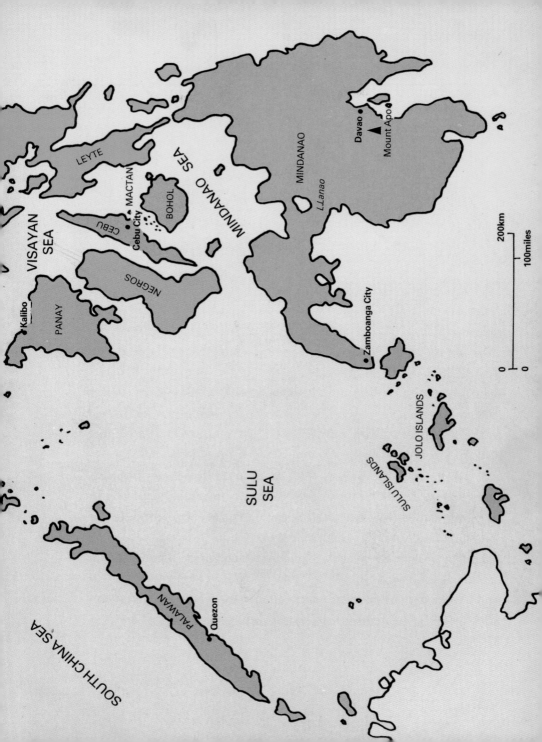

FACTS AT A GLANCE

Land and People

Official Name   Republic of the Philippines

Location   In the Pacific Ocean about 500 miles off the coast of Southeast Asia

Area   115,800 square miles (300,000 square kilometers)

Climate   Tropical; temperature varies according to the elevation

Capital   Manila

Other Cities   Quezon City, Caloocan, Davao, Cebu, Zamboanga

Population   71,539,000

Population Density   617.5 persons per square mile (238.4 persons per square kilometer)

Major Rivers   Rio Grande de Cagayan, Rio Grande de Pampanga, Rio Grande de Mindanao

Major Lakes   Laguna de Bay

Mountains   Sierra Madre, Cordillera Central

Highest Point	Mount Apo (9,692 feet / 2,954 meters)
Official Languages	Pilipino (Tagalog), English
Other Languages	Cebuano, Ilocano, Hiligaynon, Bicol
Ethnic Groups	Filipinos (mostly of Malay stock), *mestizos* (Indian mixed with Chinese, Spanish or American groups)
Religions	Roman Catholic, Protestant, Muslim, Aglipayan (Philippine Independent Church)
Literacy Rate	94 percent

Economy

Natural Resources	Gold, silver, iron ore, copper, lead, chromite, nickel, manganese, limestone
Agricultural Products	Sugarcane, rice, coconuts, corn, bananas, pineapples, tobacco
Industries	Textile, mining, processed foods
Major Imports	Mineral fuels, capital goods, cereals, chemicals
Major Exports	Electrical equipment, coconut products, clothing, fruits and vegetables, sugar products
Currency	Philippine peso

Government

Form of Government	Unitary republic
Government Bodies	Senate and House of Representatives
Formal Head of State	President

HISTORY AT A GLANCE

150,000 B.C.	A land bridge to the rest of Asia makes possible several waves of Stone Age immigrants.
5000 B.C.	The last land bridge to Asia sinks but waves of immigration continue by canoe.
960-1279 A.D.	Ships from the Chinese Sung Dynasty regularly visit the islands to trade.
800-1377	The islands are heavily influenced by the Indian kingdom of Srivijaya on Sumatra.
1293-1478	Another Indian kingdom of Indonesia, the Majapahit of Java, influences the Philippines.
1380	Islam is brought to the islands by Indian Muslim traders. The greatest success for the new religion is on the southern island of Mindanao.
1521	Ferdinand Magellan lands on the islands during his Pacific voyage and claims them for Spain. Magellan is killed soon after in a battle with local islanders.
1543	Ruy Lopez de Villalobos leads a second Spanish expedition to the islands. Although he does not succeed in establishing a permanent settlement,

10

he gives the territory its permanent name, the Philippines, originally "Filipinas," after Philip II of Spain.

1565   Miguel Lopez de Legaspi founds permanent settlement and conquers most of the islands.

1571   Legaspi occupies the village of Manila and builds Intramuros fortress. He soon conquers all of the Philippines except for the Muslim areas, Mindanao and the Sulu Islands.

1762   Manila is briefly occupied by the British during the Seven Years War.

1821   The independence of Spain's Latin American colonies leads to many changes. The islands are ruled directly from Spain, rather than Mexico City. Loss of the trade with Latin America results in decades of stagnation.

1845   The French attempt to acquire a base for operations against Vietnam, but are driven out by the Spanish.

1869   Completion of the Suez Canal makes contact with Spain easier.

1898   War breaks out between the United States and Spain. Admiral George Dewey defeats the Spanish fleet in Manila Bay (May 1). Under the Treaty of Paris (December 10) between the United States and Spain, the U.S. annexes the Philippines in return for a $20 million dollar payment. No Filipinos are allowed to be present at the negotiations.

1899   Having expected independence after the Spanish defeat, Filipinos launch attacks against American forces (February 4). Filipino forces are driven

11

away from the Manila area but the revolt, known as the Philippine Insurrection, drags on.

1902   The Moros, Muslim tribesmen of Mindanao and the southern islands, revolt against American rule.

1935   Manuel Quezon elected president of the Philippine Commonwealth, a U.S.-sponsored government that has some control over domestic affairs.

1941   Japanese forces attack the Philippines (December 8).

1942   The last American and Filipino forces surrender to the Japanese on Corregidor Island in Manila Bay on May 6. Manuel Quezon establishes a government-in-exile in Washington, D.C. on May 14.

1944   U.S. forces launch an invasion of the Japanese-occupied Philippines (October 20). They are led by General Douglas MacArthur and accompanied by Manuel Quezon.

1945   Manila is recaptured (March 3).

1946   The Philippines gain full independence from the United States. The United States maintains several large military bases on Philippine soil.

1946-1954   A communist insurrection begins in central Luzon. The rebels are gradually defeated, largely due to the efforts of defense minister Ramon Magsaysay.

1953   Magsaysay is elected president of the Philippines. The Philippines joins the Southeast Asia Treaty Organization (SEATO), consisting of the United

States, Britain, France, Australia, New Zealand, Pakistan, and Thailand.

1957 Ramon Magsaysay is killed in an airplane crash (March 17), a great loss for the nation.

1964 A new communist insurgency breaks out and drags on for 10 years.

1970 A small Muslim revolt breaks out in the southern islands.

1972 Philippine president Ferdinand Marcos uses the insurgencies and other domestic problems as an excuse to start dictatorial rule.

1975 The Ali vs Frazier world heavyweight boxing match in Manila brings international attention to the Philippines.

1976 SEATO is disbanded at ceremonies in Manila.

1983 Benigno Aquino, a major political opponent of Ferdinand Marcos, is assassinated. His wife Corazon carries on his opposition campaign. Mounting foreign and domestic pressure causes Marcos to announce new elections (1985).

1986 Corazon Aquino defeats Ferdinand Marcos for the presidency. Marcos flees the country. The Aquino administration is unable to carry out many of the reforms it had planned.

1991 U.S. bases in the Philippines are closed. The naval base at Subic Bay is later heavily damaged by the volcanic eruption of Mt. Pinatubo.

1992 Former defense minister and Aquino supporter Fidel Ramos is elected president. He vows to carry on reform programs.

1

Mabuhay!

The Philippines is one of the most interesting and unusual countries in the Far East. Not only is it made up of some seven thousand islands but it is also the only Christian nation in Asia.

Its people, the Filipinos, are a good-looking race related to the Malays and the Indonesians. However, unlike their Muslim brothers, they are mainly Christians with the majority being Roman Catholic by faith. There are thus thousands of churches in the Philippines. It is only in the Muslim south that mosques and minarets can be seen.

What is unusual, too, is that many Filipinos have Spanish names. The Spanish language, though, is not widely spoken in the Philippines. Instead, the Filipinos take great pride in being the third largest English-speaking people in the world.

Unlike its Asian neighbors, the Philippines has a unique culture which is a blend of Malay, Indian, Chinese, Spanish and American influences. This fascinating mixture of Asian and Western cultures, customs, traditions and way of life has

A group of islands in the Philippines, seen from the air.

certainly made the Philippines a land where East meets West.

Just where is the Philippines? It lies at the western rim of the Pacific Ocean about 500 miles (805 kilometers) off the coast of Southeast Asia. Situated north of the Equator, between latitudes 4 degrees North and 21 degrees North, it is made up of some seven thousand islands and islets.

About one-third of the islands have names; many of the rest are either rocks or coral reefs. Less than one thousand islands are inhabited. Only eleven of them make up about ninety-six percent of the total land area of the Philippines.

This archipelago of tropical islands is scattered over a distance of 1,100 miles (1,800 kilometers) from north to south. It roughly forms a triangle with the Batanes Islands in the north

15

as its topmost point, and the Sulu Islands and the island of Mindanao in the south as its base.

Two of the largest islands are Luzon in the north and Mindanao in the south. Luzon has an area of 40,420 square miles (104,687 square kilometers) while Mindanao has an area of 36,537 square miles (94,631 square kilometers). Between them, in the Visayan Sea, are the islands known as the Visayas. They include the larger and more important islands of Samar, Masbate, Leyte, Bohol, Cebu, Negros and Panay. To the west are the Calamian Islands and the long, narrow island of Palawan. In the extreme south are the Sulu Islands which stretch out like stepping-stones between the Zamboanga peninsula of Mindanao and the Malaysian state of Sabah on the island of Borneo.

To the north of the Philippines lies the island of Taiwan. To its south are Borneo and the islands of Indonesia. Across the South China Sea to the west lies the southeastern coast of Asia. To the east is the Pacific Ocean—the largest ocean in the world, stretching over one-third of the earth's surface to the western shores of North and South America.

Named in the sixteenth century after King Philip II of Spain, the Philippines was a Spanish colony for almost three and a half centuries. This explains why even today most of the people have Spanish names and are Roman Catholics. Their manners, culture and buildings also reflect the long years of Spanish influence. To this day, the country's currency is the *peso* which is made up of one hundred *centavos*. The words *peso* and *centavo*

A wooden religious carving, dating from the Spanish occupation.

both come from the Spanish language as do many other words used in the Philippines today.

Fifty years of American rule, in the first half of the twentieth century, has given the Philippines its American system of education and its style of democracy. It was at this time that the use of the English language became widespread, and American music, basketball, hamburgers and hotdogs gained wide popularity.

17

The Philippines became independent from the United States on July 4, 1946, after the Second World War. It then became officially known as the *Republika ng Pilipinas*—the Republic of the Philippines.

Numerous local languages and dialects are spoken in the Philippines but Pilipino has become the country's national language. Pilipino is based on *Tagalog*, a local language spoken in central Luzon.

A Pilipino word that visitors to the Philippines soon learn is the greeting *Mabuhay*! (pronounced Ma-bu-high). It means "to live," that is, to enjoy life to the full. Often used by the cheerful and friendly Filipinos, *Mabuhay* has come to mean "Hello," "Cheers!" or simply "Welcome to the Philippines!"

2

Exploring the Philippines

Because of its thousands of islands, the Philippines coastline is one of the longest in the world. The country's irregular shape has also provided it with numerous peninsulas, islets, bays, gulfs and straits and as many as sixty-one natural harbors. Manila Bay, in Luzon, is among one of the world's finest natural harbors. On its eastern shore stands Manila, the nation's capital.

The influence of the sea is widely felt throughout the Philippines—in its climate as well as in the way of life of the islanders. The sea is warm, clear, calm and gentle as it washes the white, sandy beaches of many of the Philippine islands. It is fierce and violent when churned up by tropical storms.

The waters between the islands are not deep and are easily crossed when there are no storms. The sea to the west of the Philippines is more shallow than the much deeper waters of the Pacific to the east. This has led to the popular belief that the Philippine Islands were once part of the continent of Asia,

A general view of modern Manila.

separated from it hundreds of thousands of years ago by the rise in sea level after the Ice Ages. This theory has been used to explain why a number of plants and animals found in the Philippines are similar to those in Southeast Asia.

Another theory states that the islands are of volcanic origin, and that the eruption of underwater volcanoes during prehistoric times lifted the ocean floor so that the tops of submarine mountains jutted out of the sea to form the islands. Even now some islands still rise or sink during volcanic eruptions.

What do the Filipinos themselves say about the origin of their islands? An ancient legend tells the story of a bird that once flew over a world that had only sea and sky. There was no land on which the poor bird could rest. Tired, and in great need of a resting-place, the bird started a quarrel between the sea and the sky. In no time at all, the sea's angry waves were lashing out at the sky. Then the furious sky threw huge rocks down into the sea. These rocks became the world's first land—the Philippines. And here the grateful bird came to rest.

Most of the larger islands of the Philippines have a rugged land mass with mountains running in the same general direction as the islands—from north to south. The highest peak is Mount Apo in Mindanao. It is an active volcano, rising to a height of 9,690 feet (2,954 meters) above sea level. Mount Pulog, sacred to the tribes in the northwestern mountain range of Luzon, is about 9,600 feet (2,926 meters) high. Mount Mayon, however, is the most famous of the mountains in the

Part of the central mountain range on Luzon.

Philippines. This volcano, near the town of Legazpi in southeastern Luzon, has the world's most perfect cone. Although beautiful to look at, Mayon is considered by the Filipinos to be the "angriest" volcano. Its history includes a record number of eruptions, the most recent being in 1978.

The most interesting volcano in the Philippines is Taal. It is believed to be the lowest volcano in the world. Situated in the middle of Lake Taal, south of Manila, it has another and deeper lake within its own crater. Taal's occasional eruptions have caused much destruction in the surrounding area.

The Philippines has some fifty volcanoes, at least ten of which are active. They are located along a major fault zone (where the layers of rock are broken) which runs across the archipelago from Lingayen Gulf on the western coast of Luzon

Mount Mayon in southeastern Luzon. This spectacular mountain is the world's most perfectly shaped volcanic cone.

to Leyte in the Visayas and then south through eastern Mindanao. This zone is part of the "chain of fire" that runs along the borders of the Pacific Ocean—from the Aleutian Islands (off Alaska) down to Tierra del Fuego (at the tip of the South American Continent) and up to New Zealand, Indonesia, the Philippines and Japan. Four-fifths of the world's active volcanoes are found along this "chain of fire."

Earthquakes are common in the Philippines but many are too weak to be felt. Fortunately, severe earthquakes and tidal waves, such as the one which killed more than five thousand people in 1976, do not happen frequently.

Along the fault zone, to the east of Mindanao Island, lies the Mindanao Trench. At 34,218 feet (10,670 meters), it is six times deeper than the Grand Canyon in the United States. Only one other spot on the ocean floor is deeper, and that is the Mariana Trench which lies off the island of Guam in the Pacific.

Lowlands are scarce in the Philippines. The most important is the Central Plain of Luzon, north of Manila, which is the main rice-producing area of the Philippines. Other lowlands are formed by valleys and by the narrow coastal plains of the numerous islands.

A vast system of rivers flow through the plains and valleys. They not only irrigate the land but also serve as waterways. The longest rivers in Luzon are the Rio Grande de Cagayan, the Rio Grande de Pampanga and the Agno. Those of Mindanao include the Agusan and the Rio Grande de Mindanao. *Rio Grande* is the Spanish for "great river."

A farmer preparing a rice paddy on the Central Plain of Luzon.

Because of its high rainfall, the Philippines has a larger number of lakes, rushing mountain streams and cascading waterfalls. Its largest lake is Laguna de Bay, southeast of Manila. Laguna de Bay (Bay of Laguna) is not a bay as its name suggests. It is actually a lake. Shaped like a fractured heart, it covers an area of some 350 square miles (900 square kilometers). It was so named by the earliest Spaniards who may have been deceived by its enormous size.

To the southeast of Laguna de Bay is the well-known Pagsanjan Falls—the favorite destination of tourists who want to experience the thrill of "shooting the rapids" with local boatmen in their long, narrow *bancas* or flat-bottomed boats.

Yet another interesting area in the Philippines is the Chocolate Hills of Bohol. Bohol is the island to the east of Cebu

24

Island in the central Visayas. The Chocolate Hills, found in the center of Bohol, consist of hundreds of rounded, grass-covered mounds. These mounds—the result of erosion—are between 300 and 1,000 feet (100 and 300 meters) in height. They are green for several months of the year. During the hot, dry season, the grass turns brown—hence the name Chocolate Hills. According to a local legend, these hills were formed when huge teardrops fell from the eyes of an unhappy, weeping giant.

The Philippines also has one famous man-made landmark. This is the Banaue rice terraces, north of Mount Pulog, in northwestern Luzon. These rice terraces, 6,000 feet (1,800 meters) up in the Luzon mountains, were built more than two thousand years ago by the Ifugao tribe. It is their sturdy, tanned descendants who cultivate the rice terraces today.

The Banaue rice terraces.

Looking like giant staircases, the green and brown rice terraces encircle whole mountains, covering an area of some 4,000 square miles (10,360 square kilometers). They are an awe-inspiring sight, especially bearing in mind the primitive tools used to carve them out of the rugged mountain slopes. To the Filipinos, the Banaue rice terraces are easily the eighth wonder of the world.

The Philippines has a tropical climate which is generally hot and humid all year round. There are two distinct seasons—the dry and the wet—but, because no part of any island is very far from the sea, temperatures are fairly even throughout the archipelago. The average temperature is about 81 degrees Fahrenheit (27 degrees Celsius), except in the mountains where it is much cooler.

Rainfall is heavy. Its distribution, however, is uneven because the mountain ranges act as natural barriers against the rain-bearing monsoons or seasonal winds. The Northeast Monsoon blows between the months of December and May; the Southwest Monsoon between June and November.

Typhoons are another source of rainfall. They are fierce tropical storms that blow in from the Pacific bringing with them strong winds and heavy rainfall. The Philippines is one of the most typhoon-prone areas in the world. An average of about twenty typhoons hit the northern and central parts of the Philippines every year, especially between the months of August and October. Known locally as *bagyos,* these typhoons cause disastrous floods, damage to property and loss of life.

The abundant rainfall and constant heat have given rise to a great variety of plant life in the Philippines. There are orchids and many species of other flowering plants as well as dense, evergreen forests. Along the coasts are the mangrove swamps and coconut groves while many species of pines grow on the mountain slopes. In between grow bamboo, banana trees, palms such as the sago, nipah and betel and other trees valued for their timber.

Most of the animals found in the Philippines are not large, but are similar to those found in Southeast Asia. The more numerous ones include deer, wild pigs, wild cats (civets), mongooses, otters and monkeys. An animal most commonly seen helping the farmer in his field is the *carabao* or water buffalo which is also found in most parts of southern Asia.

Some of the world's strangest animals are also found in the Philippines. There is the *tamarao* which looks like a small water buffalo, although it has horns and is very wild and dangerous. It is found only in the dense jungles on the highlands of Mindoro Island which lies due south of Manila Bay.

The *tarsier* is a small monkey with a head and body measuring about six inches (fifteen centimeters). It has a long tail and large eyes. Its head can make a 180-degree turn to look at whatever is directly behind it. The *tarsier* lives high up in the trees, coming out only at night to hunt smaller animals for food. *Tarsiers* are found on islands of volcanic origin, mainly in the forests of Bohol, Leyte, Samar and Mindanao.

There are also many species of butterflies, insects, lizards and snakes and at least 750 species of birds. Unique among the birds is the monkey-eating eagle known as the *haribon*. It is found only in the mountain range in the northeastern part of Luzon, and in some parts of Mindanao and Palawan. It has a wing-span of some six feet (1.8 meters) and is said to be the largest and fiercest eagle in the world.

The warm, clear seas around the Philippine islands contain a rich variety of seafood, corals, shells and tropical fish. The Sulu Sea in the far south is famous for its pearls and its many varieties of beautiful and rare sea shells which are widely sought by collectors from all over the world.

The tiny tersier—the most famous of the monkeys of the Philippines.

A craftsman using shells to create objects of beauty to sell to visitors from abroad.

The world's smallest fish, believed to be found nowhere else on earth, swim in Lake Buhi, not far from Mount Mayon in southeastern Luzon. These tiny fish are called *tabios*. They are very small—about the size of a grain of rice—and are very difficult to see.

The Philippines is divided into seventy-three provinces, with the smallest unit in each province being the village. Life in the rural areas and in the villages has not changed much over the years. Agriculture, along with fishing and forestry, provides a living for the people.

The island of Luzon, in the north, has most of the cultivated

29

lands. It is also the most densely populated island. Mindanao, in the south, is the least developed.

Although the Philippines has some large estates growing crops such as rice, sugarcane and coconuts, most of the farms are small. The hard life and poverty of peasant farmers in many areas have resulted in a steady drift of people, especially the young, to the cities to look for work. This has led to problems of unemployment and the growth of slum areas in the cities, especially in Manila.

Manila, the present capital, is the most important city in the Philippines. It is the seat of government and the nerve center of the nation. It began as a port and trading center at the mouth of the Pasig River which flows from Laguna de Bay into Manila Bay. Today, it covers an area of something like 245 square miles (635 square kilometers) along the eastern shore of Manila Bay, on both sides of the Pasig River.

This vast, developed area is now known as Metropolitan Manila or Metro Manila for short. It includes the cities of Manila, Caloocan, Quezon, Pasay and thirteen other towns. It is certainly the largest and most densely populated urban area in the Philippines. About ten million people live in Metro Manila.

The fifth largest city in the Philippines is Cebu City on the island of Cebu in the central Visayas. It has the distinction of being the nation's oldest city. The cross planted by the Portuguese explorer Ferdinand Magellan in 1521 is Cebu's most famous historical landmark. Today, Cebu City is the "Queen City of the South," second only to Manila as a trading and

Magellan's Cross, now housed in a church. As well as commemorating the explorer, it is Cebu's most historic landmark.

educational center. It has a population of about 700,000 people. Its most well-known export is its handmade guitars.

Davao, at the head of Davao Gulf in the southeastern part of Mindanao Island, is the fourth largest city in the Philippines. It is the center of Mindanao's agricultural, logging and mining industries. It is more famous, though, for its fruits such as pomelos, bananas, mangosteens and especially durians, considered by many an Asian as the "king" of all tropical fruits.

Baguio, 155 miles (96 kilometers) north of Manila, is the nation's summer capital. It is 5,000 feet (1,500 meters) up in the mountains, and is cool all the year round. It is certainly the place to escape to when temperatures in Manila soar to 100 degrees

Fahrenheit (38 degrees Celsius) during the hot, dry months of April and May.

Many other cities and towns are scattered throughout the Philippines. To visit those in the north is like taking a step back in time into the Spanish colonial past. They boast beautiful Spanish-style churches and houses, as well as narrow, cobbled streets that lead onto spacious Spanish *plazas* or town squares.

In the far south, cities become more Muslim in character with their mosques and minarets. Muslim *vintas* are also a common sight in the southern seas. They are light, wooden, double-rigged boats

Coconuts. The fleshy outer pod is stripped away and discarded to reveal the more familiar coconut.

Vintas, outrigger canoes with their distinctive sails.

with colorful sails. The Muslims of Mindanao use these boats for fishing and trading.

3

The Story of the Philippines

The ancestors of the Filipino people came from Asia. They came over a period of many thousands of years. The earliest arrivals were probably cavemen hunters who followed game across South China over land bridges which at that time joined the Philippines to the continent of Asia.

The Negritos—a short and dark-skinned people with thick, curly hair—are generally believed to be the first inhabitants of the Philippines. They led a nomadic life, moving from place to place to gather food or hunt animals with their spears. Their descendants can still be found in the remote mountainous areas of islands such as Luzon, Palawan and Panay.

Other aboriginal tribes came many years later. Among them were the first farmers who cleared the forests to plant crops. Each successive group drove the more primitive tribes further inland.

Long after the land bridges had sunk into the sea, bands of adventurous sailors arrived in their log canoes from the islands of the South Pacific. Others came from the coastal areas of Southeast Asia. Among them were the Indonesians and the Malays from Borneo, the Malay Peninsula and the Indonesian islands. The later Malay immigrants—brown-skinned, slim and graceful with fine features, brown eyes and straight, black hair—are the ancestors of most of today's Filipinos.

By A.D. 1500, the Malay people could be found in most of the islands of the Philippines. They lived in small, scattered communities along the coasts and at the mouth of rivers. Their settlements, known as *barangays*, consisted of related family groups living in wooden, palm-thatched huts which were built on stilts.

Each village was a separate unit, ruled by its own chief or *datu*. As the people of each village seldom cooperated with those of

A *barangay*, a type of settlement introduced by the Malay people and now common on the Philippine coastline.

other villages scattered throughout the islands, there was a great deal of fighting between *barangays*.

As early as A.D. 700, the Philippines had begun to attract traders from Japan and China. In later centuries, more Chinese traders came, along with Indians and Arabs. Soon, some of these traders settled down in the islands.

In the early fourteenth century, Arab missionaries introduced Islam, their religion, into the Sulu Archipelago and to Mindanao. This new faith helped to unite the people of the south. Given time, Islam would most probably have spread to the rest of the country as it did in Indonesia and Malaysia. But then the Spaniards appeared on the scene.

The Spaniards were the first Europeans to land in the

Mosques such as this one are now a frequent sight in the southernmost islands of the Philippines. Traders and missionaries brought Islam to this part of the world in the fourteenth century.

Philippines. An expedition, led by Ferdinand Magellan, reached Cebu in the central Visayas in 1521.

Magellan, a Portuguese explorer in the service of the Spanish King, wanted to continue the search, begun by Christopher Columbus, for the rich spice islands of the East Indies. As the route eastward via Africa and the Indian Ocean was controlled by the Portuguese, Magellan sailed west across the Atlantic, round the tip of South America and across the Pacific Ocean. He reached the islands to be known later as the Philippines, and claimed them for Spain.

Magellan did not live long to enjoy his triumph for he was killed in a fight with Chief Lapulapu of Mactan Island, just off the coast of Cebu. Unlike Rajah Humabon, the chief of Cebu, Lapulapu refused to submit to Spanish authority.

After Magellan's death, the people of the islands turned against the remaining Spaniards, forcing them to flee for their lives. Of the five ships that left Spain under Magellan's command, only one managed to return home, via the Indian Ocean and Africa. This ship was the first to sail around the world.

On Mactan Island today there are two monuments—one to Chief Lapulapu, the first Filipino to fight against foreign rule and the other to Magellan, the brave explorer.

Spain sent more expeditions to the Philippines from its colonies in Mexico (New Spain). But there was no permanent settlement until 1565 when Miguel Lopez de Legazpi established one at Cebu. Then Spanish conquests spread northward to the other

Activity at the port of Legazpi, named after Miguel Lopez Legazpi who started the first Spanish colony in the Philippines in 1565.

islands. Finally, in 1571, Legazpi captured Manila from its Muslim chief, Rajah Sulayman. Then Intramuros, the walled city of the Spaniards, was built. It was to become the center of Spanish rule in the Philippines.

With the conquering sword came the cross. The Spaniards were anxious to introduce Christianity to the Far East. Roman Catholic priests or friars converted the Filipino people, building churches and schools wherever they went. But the Spanish language was never taught to the masses. Instead, the Spanish friars learned the local dialects and used them to educate and convert the Filipinos.

By the year 1600, most of the Filipinos had accepted Spanish rule. They had also accepted the Catholic religion which they

38

happily combined with their ancient belief in the spirits of the world of Nature. The only people who successfully resisted the Spaniards were the fierce and united Muslims of the Sulu Archipelago and Mindanao. The Spaniards called these people *Moros* (Moors) after the Arab Muslims who had once conquered Spain.

Spanish rule lasted for 333 years. The Spaniards, unfortunately, were not interested in developing the islands or improving their agriculture. Besides introducing Christianity, their only other interest was in trade.

Each year, a galleon set sail from Manila carrying rich cargoes of silk, spices, precious stones and many other riches from the Orient. These "Manila galleons" sailed across the Pacific to Acapulco on the western coast of Mexico, returning with Mexican silver. This trade was to last for 250 years. It was also to remain firmly in Spanish hands, for only the Spaniards were allowed to trade. So they grew rich, together with the Chinese traders who supplied them with the precious cargoes they wanted.

Other Spaniards who served their King well were rewarded with large areas of land. The Church, too, was given land. And the land included the people living on it. This meant that the Filipinos not only had to give up their land, but also had to work for their new masters. In addition, they were heavily taxed. Life was hard and the people were no better than slaves.

The harsh Spanish rule stirred up much resentment. Revolts occurred from time to time but they were easily put down.

39

A typical rural house on Cebu Island, not dissimilar to those built at the time of the Spanish occupation.

Because of Spanish interest in trade, the islands remained largely undeveloped. There was no industry to boast of and no agricultural development.

It was not until the 1800s, when the country's economy was at its lowest, that Manila was at last opened to foreign trade. Some reforms were also introduced but they were too few and had come rather late. Discontent and growing unrest was, by now, widespread.

Among the Filipinos who wanted justice for his countrymen was Jose Rizal. Of Spanish-Filipino blood, he was the son of a

40

rich sugar planter. He had studied in Spain and he was a brilliant student. Rizal returned to the Philippines to work as a doctor, believing that reform, and not armed resistance, was the answer to his people's problems. He wrote two books, in Spanish, pointing out everything that was wrong in Philippine society and giving suggestions for changes that could be made. His writings made his fellow Filipinos more aware of themselves and their beloved country.

The Spanish government branded Rizal a traitor. On December 30, 1896, he was brought to Manila and executed by a firing-squad at the Luneta, now known as Rizal Park. He was only thirty-five years old.

Rizal's death shocked the Filipinos, stirring them into open revolt under the leadership of Emilio Aquinaldo. The revolt spread to various parts of Luzon as well as the other islands. The Spaniards, busy with another revolt in their Caribbean colony of Cuba, tried to make peace. Reforms were promised but these never came about.

In 1898, the Spanish-American War broke out over Cuba. American ships under the command of Admiral George Dewey attacked and defeated the Spanish fleet in Manila Bay. Filipinos fought alongside the Americans. They believed the Americans had come to free them from Spanish rule.

On June 12, 1898, the Philippines declared itself a republic with Aquinaldo as president. But it was not long before the Americans took over the country. In anger, the Filipinos turned against the Americans, fighting with them for almost three

years. The fighting ended in 1901 when Aquinaldo was captured.

Once again, the Philippines was in the hands of a foreign power. And, just as Spain never succeeded in controlling the Muslim south, neither did the United States.

The Americans brought in teachers and Protestant missionaries. They built schools and made education free but compulsory. English became the language of instruction. For the first time in history, the Filipino people had a common language.

Public health improved, roads and railroads were built and

42

Filipinos were given more control over their own affairs. Although things were better than they had been under Spanish rule, there was much unhappiness over trade conditions that catered more to American than Filipino needs. There was also disagreement over the date of the country's independence. The Filipinos wanted it to be soon, but the Americans wanted them to wait.

It was not until 1935 that a Commonwealth government was formed with Manuel Quezon as its first president. Full independence was to come ten years later. Unfortunately, the Second World War intervened. The United States was drawn into the war when Japan attacked Pearl Harbor in Hawaii in December 1941. Soon afterwards, the Japanese landed in the Philippines. Filipino-American forces fought bravely but were pushed back to the island of Corregidor and the Bataan Peninsula at the entrance to Manila Bay. Several months later, they surrendered, leaving the Japanese to rule the Philippines for the next three and a half years.

Although the Filipinos suffered greatly under the Japanese rulers, many continued to resist the new conquerors. The main resistance came from the Communist-led guerilla group known as the Hukbalahaps or Huks whose battle cry was "Freedom from the Japanese!" This was later changed to "Freedom from landlords!" when the Philippines became fully independent.

The return of American troops to the Philippines brought an end to the war. It also left the country in ruins. But, in spite of enormous problems, Filipino leaders pressed for independence from the United States. On July 4, 1946, the Philippines became a republic with Manuel Roxas as the first President. The Philippines thus became the first colony in Asia to be free of foreign rule.

Massive American aid was needed to rebuild the Philippines again. This was given on condition that American citizens could compete on equal terms with the Filipinos to develop the country's resources. The United States also kept two military bases in the Philippines—the Clark Air Base and the Subic Bay Naval Base.

President Manuel Roxas, who died after two years in office, was succeeded by Vice-President Elpidio Quirino. In 1948, Quirino was re-elected for the next four-year term. In 1953, Ramon Magsaysay became president after successfully putting down the Huks—the Communist champions of the landless peasants. After Magsaysay came Carlos Garcia (1957), Diosdado Macapagal (1961) and Ferdinand Marcos (1965).

It was Diosdado Macapagal who changed the Independence Day of the Philippines from July 4th to June 12th—the anniversary of the 1898 Declaration of Independence at which Aquinaldo was made president. It was Ferdinand Marcos, however, who was to remain as president for twenty years.

According to the 1935 Constitution, the Philippines is a democratic republic with an elected president, who (like the vice-president) could only serve two terms of four years each.

In 1972, just a year before his second term of office ended, Marcos declared martial law. This was because of the growing

44

A ship at the former U.S. Naval Base in Subic Bay.

violence and disorder in the country. The Communist guerrillas, now calling themselves the New People's Army (NPA) had started fighting government troops again in the late 1960s and early 1970s. Muslim guerrillas in the south had also clashed with the Christian government in their desire to be a separate, independent unit.

In 1973, Marcos drew up a new constitution that gave him more power to push through reforms, especially those regarding land ownership. Under this new constitution, he could also remain in power for an unlimited period of time. Although martial law was lifted in 1981, Marcos continued in power until February 1986 when Corazon Aquino, wife of an assassinated opposition leader, became the new president.

One of the main tasks of the president was to appoint a

45

Women washing clothes at a primitive laundry. Despite promises of a democratic government, day-to-day living remains as hard for the people of the Philippines as it ever has been.

committee to draw up a new constitution to reflect "the true aspirations of the Filipino people." This new Philippine constitution, drafted and ratified in February 1987, returned the Philippines to the democratic American-style government it used to have before Marcos imposed martial law and wrote his own constitution to establish his unlimited rule. It also limited the presidency to a single six-year term.

The Aquino administration was faced with numerous problems, such as the 1991 eruption of Mount Pinatubo, a severely depleted economy and numerous coup attempts. Aquino instituted a period of democracy that led in 1992 to the free election of her successor, Fidel V. Ramos.

46

4

The Filipino People

According to an ancient legend, the first Filipino and his feminine counterpart, the Filipina, came into being at the same time. Both emerged from a bamboo trunk that had been split open by a huge bird.

Yet another story that Filipinos love to tell explains how man was made. A long time ago, when the world was young, the creator god shaped man from a lump of clay and put him into an oven to bake. In his eagerness to see how man would turn out, the god took him out of the oven too soon, resulting in the making of a pale, white man. In a second attempt, man was left too long in the oven and came out dark-skinned, almost black. In a third attempt, the timing was just right and so was created the perfectly golden, brown-skinned man—the Filipino.

Interesting as these traditional stories may be, we need to go back to the study of history to find out who the Filipinos are and where they come from. As we already know, many different races—Asians as well as Westerners—came to settle in the

Philippines. Many came as settlers, others as conquerors.

Although descended mainly from the Malays, today's Filipinos are made up of a fascinating mixture of races. Many have physical features and skin coloring that is the result of intermarriage between native-born Filipinos and other racial groups that have settled in the Philippines throughout its history—the Chinese, Arabs, Indians, Spaniards, Americans, Japanese and later, other Europeans.

Many people are the descendants of Filipinos married to Spaniards. Then, there are the descendants of Filipinos married to the Chinese or later, the Americans. Known as *mestizos* (people of mixed race), these descendants are usually fairer than their fellow Filipinos, often with the best features inherited from either one or both parents.

The varying origins of the Filipino people are evident in this group of friends who are descended from differing races.

Some Mexicans who settled in the Philippines during the 250-year period of the "Manila galleon" trade, also added an Aztec-Spanish strain to the racial composition of the people. As there is no prejudice against mixed marriages in the Philippines, it is not surprising to find that some Filipinos are fair, some dark while others are in-between.

Not all Filipinos, however, are of mixed ancestry. A small number are the descendants of ancestors who came to the Philippines long before the Spaniards set foot on the islands. These people, known as the country's "cultural minorities" can still be found scattered throughout the Philippines. They make up at least ten percent of the country's present population.

Among them are the curly-haired, dark-skinned Negritos, believed to be the original inhabitants of the Philippines. Small numbers of them making up tribes such as the Aeta, Ati and Agta, can be found living in the mountain jungles of the islands of Palawan, Panay, Negros, Leyte, Samar and Luzon.

Then there are the mountain peoples of northern Luzon, known collectively as the Igorots. They consist of five main tribes—the Ifugaos whose ancestors built the Banaue rice terraces, the Bontocs who today combine their ancient religion with the teachings of American missionaries, the Benguets, the Kalingas and the Apayaos. Their retreat into the remote mountainous areas of northern Luzon, when successive waves of settlers and conquerors came to the Philippines, kept generations of their people beyond outside influence.

The Muslims or *Moros* of Mindanao and the Sulu Archipelago

form the largest minority group. They are believed to number about five million. Although of the same Malay race as the majority of Filipinos, they have a long history of hostile and aggressive behavior. Their religion is different. So is the way they dress and the way they live.

Among the most interesting tribes of Muslims are the Badjao, the Maranao and the Tausug. The Badjao are sea gypsies who spend their entire lives on their floating boat homes. They are the true "wanderers of the Sulu Seas." The Maranao are the people of Lake Lanao on Mindanao. They are very artistic. Their brass containers, wood-carvings and brightly colored *malongs* (tubular women's dresses) are well-known. So is their quarrelsome nature which has led to many generations of blood feuds. The Tausug or "people of the current" form the main group of Muslims in the south. They live on the island of Jolo in the Sulu Archipelago and around the port of Zamboanga in the southwestern part of Mindanao. They are fiercely independent. Their ancestors were the first Filipinos to become Muslims.

There are other minority groups living in the south. They include some non-Muslim tribes who live in the remote highlands of Mindanao. Among them are the Tiruray, a horseriding people of southwestern Mindanao and the T'boli, a tribe living near Lake Cibu in the Cotabato province of Mindanao.

Although the majority of Filipinos share a common Malay heritage, they display many differences in character and temperament. The Filipinos of northern Luzon are, in general, considered to be shrewd and hard-working. Those from central and

Filipino Muslims in their distinctive traditional dress.

southern Luzon are more enterprising and seem to be happiest when in the company of others. The Visayans are well-known for their usually kind and generous nature while the most feared Filipinos are the Muslims of the south. They have the reputation of being more sensitive and quick-tempered and ready to draw out their knives at the slightest provocation.

Filipinos from different parts of the Philippines also have a variety of manners, customs, attitudes and values. This variety, together with the physical differences between the Filipinos themselves, have not divided the people as much as the different dialects that they speak.

Although Filipino dialects belong to the same Malayan-Polynesian language group, they are so varied that they have often been classified as different languages. It is said that some

51

Filipino schoolchildren in class.

seventy-seven or more local languages are spoken in the Philippines. The government recognizes two official languages today. They are Pilipino and English. Pilipino, based on *Tagalog*, is the country's national language. Pilipino is taught today in Philippine schools; it is hoped that the greater use of Pilipino will help to strengthen the bond among the Filipino people.

English, introduced into the Philippines by the American administration, has been the sole language of instruction in schools for seventy years. It is thus widely spoken in the Philippines and is the language used in business and administration.

Spanish, never taught to the masses during Spain's 333-year rule, is spoken by only a very small minority today. These are usually the members of old-established families. Spanish is taught today in the universities.

Education is very important to the Filipinos. All parents dream of sending their children to school and, if possible, to a university. Unfortunately, with about seventy percent of the population believed to be living below the poverty line, this dream is not easy to realize.

Children in the rural areas have to help out on the farm and at home from an early age. Even among the poor living in the cities, many have to give up schooling in order to work to support their families. And Filipino families are not small. They are large, and made up of at least three generations living together.

The first six years of schooling is free for all Filipino children. It is also compulsory. Reading, writing, arithmetic and other subjects are taught in Pilipino and in English. Government

One generation of a typically large Filipino family.

primary (elementary) schools are found in cities, towns and almost every village in the Philippines.

The next four years of education is provided by secondary (high) schools, most of which are run by Catholic religious orders. For those who are able to afford further education, there are about fifty state-run universities and colleges.

The most famous university in the Philippines is the University of Santo Tomas in Manila. It was founded in 1611 by the Roman Catholic Church. The oldest is the University of San Carlos in Cebu City, founded in 1595. The best is said to be the

A young child working on the family farm.

A contemporary
engraving of Ferdinand
Magellan, the explorer.

University of the Philippines which is supported by the
government. It was established in Manila in 1908 and moved to
Quezon City in 1948.

The Philippines is the only Christian nation in Asia. Eighty-
three percent of the population are Roman Catholics while at
least another five percent are Protestants. Christianity was
introduced into the Philippines by the Spaniards during the
sixteenth century. The first European to arrive at Cebu in
the central Visayas was Magellan. He and his men came carrying

the cross and the sword. What won the day for him, the story goes, was not his offer of friendship nor the sight of Spanish ships and weapons, but rather the native queen's first look at the statue of the Christ Child. It melted her heart, making her promise to let the *Santo Nino* (Holy Child) of the Spaniards take the place of the gods and the spirits worshipped by her people.

This incident was vividly described by Francesco Antonio Pigafetta, a historian, who was with Magellan, in these words: "*After dinner the priest and many of us went ashore to try to baptize the queen of Cebu. While the priest was getting ready the rites, I showed her an image of our Lord, a little statue of the infant Jesus. When she saw it, she was deeply touched and, crying, asked to be baptized. The queen wanted the image to take the place of her idols, so I gave it to her.*"

When Magellan was killed soon afterwards, the islanders returned to their old religion. But, some forty years later, when other Spaniards returned to colonize the Philippines, Spanish priests set out in earnest to convert the people. Thus began the Filipinos' introduction to a personal relationship with God.

Many Filipinos accepted the Catholic faith of the Spanish priests because they found Christianity emotionally appealing. The strong belief in their gods and spirits, however, could not easily be denied. These spirits were eventually to be transformed in their eyes into angels, saints and devils.

Today, the Catholic religion in the Philippines is marked by many colorful festivals and processions. Every town has its Catholic church and its own special images of the Virgin Mary and Baby Jesus. Each home, too, has its own altar with those

56

images. Church holidays are well observed as are the special days of patron saints. It was only in the early twentieth century, when the Americans took over the Philippines, that Protestant missionaries came to the islands to preach the gospel. They won a number of converts.

The largest group of non-Christians in the Philippines are the Muslims of the south. They form about four percent of the population. Muslims believe that Allah is the one true God and that Muhammad is His prophet. Their holy book is the Koran.

Islam, the religion of the Muslims, started in Arabia during the seventh century A.D. Arab traders and missionaries brought the religion to the Far East when they came to trade, and later to settle. The Philippines forms the eastern limit of the spread of their religion.

Islam was introduced into the Sulu Archipelago and Mindanao almost two hundred years before the coming of the Spaniards. The religion united the people of the south, making it possible for them to resist the Spaniards and, later, the Americans. Unfortunately, it has also divided them from the majority of Christian Filipinos of today.

Other non-Christians are the small groups of Filipino tribes who still practice the animist beliefs of their ancestors. Animists believe that as well as man having a soul, animals and things have souls too. Thus their world is full of the souls or spirits of ancestors, animals, streams, rocks and trees as well as of spirits without bodies. These spirits may be good or evil.

Animists also believe that for people to get along in life,

offerings have to be made to the numerous spirits, the sun, moon, stars, the powerful creator god Bathala, and a host of other gods and goddesses. As offerings can be placed anywhere—on a rock, beneath a tree or beside a stream according to where each spirit lived—temples or places of worship are not needed. It was only with the spread of Islam in the south and, later, Christianity in the central and northern Philippines that mosques and churches were built.

Early tribal artists made figures of clay. They also carved figures out of wood. The best known wood-carvings come from the mountain tribes of northern Luzon. Later, with the spread of Christianity, the carving of *santos*, figures of Catholic saints, became popular.

Tribal groups also produce attractive beadwork, mats and

A Catholic church in Iloilo.

woven fabrics of Muslim and non-Muslim design. Popular with collectors and shoppers are their brass gongs, jewelry and containers of every kind as well as their knives and elaborately-carved weapons.

Visitors to the Philippines are often dazzled by the variety of things they can buy. These are produced in the cottage industries found throughout the islands. There are beautiful wooden articles such as bowls and dishes for the home, macrame flower-pot holders and embroidered shirts, dresses, tablecloths and placemats. The eye is caught by colorful lampshades, by windchimes made of shell, and by the various types of hats, trays and basketwork made from bamboo, rattan, nipah and other palms. Beautiful jewelry is also available in shell, silver, mother-of-pearl, tortoiseshell, wood and vine as well as coral. And what is most important to the shopper—prices are among the lowest in Southeast Asia!

The Filipinos are a very artistic people as can be seen from the things they make. Their houses, too, are interesting, ranging from Malay huts on stilts to Spanish-style houses and mansions. Later buildings of the American period were more streamlined and functional while newer buildings of today are more individual and tropical in style.

Nowhere is Filipino art more visible than in the colorful *jeepneys* (public transport vehicles) that ply the streets. These *jeepneys* have often been described as a "riot of pop-art design." The gaudy and colorful *jeepney,* painted in bright colors and covered with stickers, streamers and other dazzling accessories, has become a

One of the many colorful jeepneys to be found on the roads in the Philippines—today they are manufactured in the islands.

symbol of the Philippines in modern times. They were originally army surplus jeeps left behind by the American forces after the Second World War. But they were remade to carry ten passengers or more. Today, these *jeepneys* are manufactured in the Philippines. *Jeepney* factories are often on the list of places for tourists to visit.

A ride in a *jeepney,* especially for a first-time visitor, is best done with eyes closed. Otherwise the excitement would be too much, given the Filipino drivers' happy-go-lucky spirit and the many distractions that often divert attention from the road.

Besides art and craft, Filipinos seem to have a natural talent for music. With their wonderful sense of rhythm, they are certainly the most sought-after musicians in Asia. Their music is a beautiful, harmonious blend of Filipino and Western influences.

Hand-in-hand with music, comes dance. Filipino dances draw upon the richness of early Malay folk-dances, traditional Muslim dances and Spanish dances. These Filipino dances are widely appreciated today through the efforts of the famous Bayanihan Dance Company which has performed in many countries throughout the world. Among the most well-known Filipino dance is the Singkil or Muslim "bamboo" dance.

Then, there is drama which is often linked to music and dance.

Members of the Bayanihan Dance Company giving a performance.

The Filipinos are natural performers, taking to the stage easily when plays were introduced into the Philippines from the West. The favorites are the religious passion plays as well as comedies, tragedies and sentimental dramas. When the movie theaters were introduced in the early twentieth century, the Philippines became Hollywood's second largest market. Today, fine films in Pilipino are produced. They feature modern themes to win over audiences who prefer Western films.

Filipinos are very fond of expressing themselves in poetic language. In the early days, this took the form of poems, songs, myths, legends and folk-tales. By word of mouth, these poems and stories were handed down through the generations. Out of this oral tradition grew Filipino literature. The first printed books were written in Spanish. Today, Filipino literature is written in both Pilipino and English.

5

How the Filipinos Live

Strong family ties make it quite usual in the Philippines for parents and their children, grandparents, aunts, uncles and other relatives to live together under one roof. Filipinos consider it important to keep in touch with relatives on both sides of the family. Hence families are very closely knit and always ready to celebrate happy occasions or to give help to each other during times of need.

Filipino women have always held a high position in the family. They have, since early times, been its central force. Grandparents, godparents and other elders are treated with great respect. Children are much loved.

From an early age, children are taught to obey and respect their parents, grandparents and those older than themselves. They are given a lot of freedom but, when old enough, are expected to help either on the farm or in the home. An older child looks after a younger one, with the eldest child expected to look after younger brothers and sisters should the need arise. By

This woman is a key figure in her family. Filipino society regards women very highly.

the age of twelve or thirteen, a boy is able to shoulder many family responsibilities while a girl can cook, sew and look after the home.

Traditionally, it is the custom for a young girl to ask her father's permission before going out with the young man she hopes eventually to marry. The young man, when courting his young lady, usually serenades her. With friends to help him, he plays the guitar or sings under her window in the hope of being allowed into the house. Outings are usually chaperoned by a married or older woman relative.

64

People in the rural areas tend to marry young. Those in the city, more independent and modern in outlook than their country cousins, prefer to finish their education and start on a career before settling down.

Many married couples in the Philippines have a large number of children. This is especially true of rural folk, most of whom are farmers. Extra pairs of hands are always needed to plow the fields or bring in the harvest. In 1966, the population of the Philippines was thirty-three million. By 1980, it had increased to

A woman playing a home-made stringed instrument during one of her few times of relaxation.

forty-eight million. In 1997, the population was almost seventy-two million.

The majority of Filipinos live in rural villages called *barangays* or *barrios*. Barrio is the Spanish word for village. It is also used to mean a neighborhood in the city. At the beginning of the twentieth century, more than three-quarters of the population lived in rural areas. Over the years, this figure has dropped as more young Filipinos have moved to the cities to look for work.

Dreams and hopes are not always realized and as young people move into the cities, unemployment builds up and slum neighborhoods grow. Modern life also has a strong effect on the young who are often caught in the age-old struggle between traditional values learned within the family circle and the more recent values of social change.

Change comes more slowly in rural areas where needs remain simple. Although poor, people in the *barrios* can build their own homes, grow their own food or catch fish to eat. Most villages find their standard of living sufficient for their basic needs. But hard though life can be for the poor, both in the countryside and in the cities, family ties continue to be strong.

Filipinos, who are warm-hearted and generous by nature, go to great lengths to help a relative. Friends, too, are not left out. To Filipinos, family and friends are the greatest source of strength. Similarly, hospitality to strangers is well-known, especially in rural areas where traditional values are strongly upheld.

Because of the hot and humid climate in the Philippines, light cotton clothes are usually worn. Western-style clothes are

An area typical of the slums which accommodate the steady stream of people who come from the rural areas into the cities.

popular except in minority areas where traditional clothes are worn.

Jeans and T-shirts are the favorite clothes of the young. People living in large cities such as Manila, Cebu and Davao are, of course, more fashion conscious than those from the smaller towns and villages.

The Filipino's national costume is the *barong tagalog*. This is a loose, heavily-embroidered shirt worn over the trousers. It has a closed collar with short sleeves for day wear or long, cuffed sleeves for formal occasions. No tie is worn with the *barong tagalog* which is popular with both rich and poor alike. Made in many different types of material, its price can vary, depending on

67

whether the shirt is made of low-quality fiber or the most expensive banana or pineapple fiber.

The Filipina's national costume is the *terno*, a long dress with puff sleeves. Women also wear the *kimona*. This consists of an embroidered blouse worn over a long skirt.

The Filipina's favorite flower, worn in her hair or on her dress, is the *sampaguita*. These small white jasmine flowers give out a lovely fragrance. According to folklore, the name *sampaguita* came from a lover's promise: "*Sumpaquita na di lilimutin*" meaning "To you I pledge my love, to be true always." In the folktale, the young woman who pledges her love dies of a broken heart when her young man is killed in battle. From her grave grows the jasmine shrub with its heart-shaped leaves and tiny, fragrant, white flowers. Since then, the story goes, the beautiful *sampaguita* has been cherished as the national flower of the Philippines.

Filipino food is a mixture of influences from Spanish, Chinese and Indian cooking. The result is food which is quite unlike the hot, spicy dishes of its Asian neighbors.

Rice is the staple food of the Philippines. It is served with various dishes at every meal. Fish and other seafood form the main part of the diet, either steamed, cooked lightly in spices or served with rich sauces. A popular Filipino dish is *adobo*. It consists of either chicken or pork simmered gently in oil after the meat is seasoned with vinegar, soy sauce, garlic and spices. *Lechon*, a suckling pig roasted over a charcoal fire, is the most important dish at any Filipino feast or celebration. Meals, when served local style, are eaten with the fingers.

68

A Mindanao islander in traditional dress.

Dessert consists of many types of cakes and sweets made from rice-flour, sugar and coconut. Fruits are plentiful. There are mangoes, papayas, bananas and watermelons as well as guavas, rambutans and durians from the south. A popular drink is *tuba* or coconut wine. It is made from the sap of the coconut palm. Mild and sweet when fresh, it can become intoxicating when left to ferment for a few days.

A favorite Filipino snack is *balut*. It is a duck's egg with an unhatched duckling inside. Duck eggs hatch in about twenty-eight days. The *balut* is eaten after eighteen days. It is boiled for a few minutes and them swallowed in several gulps. Many *balut* stalls can be found at dusk, in the streets of Manila.

Traditionally, meals are prepared by the women and eaten at home. Nowadays, especially in the cities, more and more meals are eaten in restaurants or at food centers or street stalls. The *turo-turo* is a Filipino modern version of a fast-food eating place. The word *turo* means "point" which is exactly what the customers do at the *turo-turo*—they simply point to whatever local dishes they want to order for their meal.

A market fruit stall.

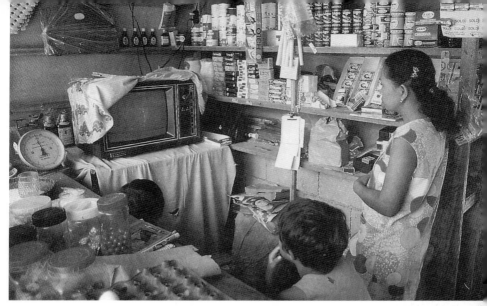

A small shop where preserved and canned food can be bought; fresh food is usually purchased from a market in the Philippines.

What do Filipino children and adults do during their leisure hours?

The children play *piko* which is a kind of hopscotch. Another favorite game is *sipa* which means "kick." The game is something like volleyball except that a hollow wicker ball is used. Feet, legs, and knees are used to kick this wicker ball over the net.

Filipino children are also very fond of basketball. It is often played in the square in front of the church, in school or wherever an improvised court can be hastily set up. Every schoolboy nourishes the hope of becoming his country's basketball star one day. This passion for basketball has made the Filipinos the top players in Asia. Even though basketball seems to be the tall man's

71

A casual game of basketball.

game, the Filipino simply uses his skill and speed to make up for his lack of height.

A popular sport with male adults in the provinces is cockfighting. On Sundays and public holidays, proud owners can be seen heading for the cockpits, carrying their prize roosters in the crook of their arms. These cockpits can be found in practically every corner of the archipelago. They are always crowded and a great deal of betting takes place during each cockfight.

Jai alai (pelota) is a fast, exciting game introduced into the Philippines from the Basque region in Spain. It is played in a long, enclosed court which has a granite wall at one end. It is similar to squash except that the hard rubber ball is caught by a player wearing a crescent-shaped wicker basket called a *cesta*. The *cesta* is tightly laced to the player's right hand. Each bout of this "game of a thousand thrills," where the ball can reach speeds of 150 miles (240 kilometers) an hour, lasts about ten minutes.

Jai alai is a popular spectator sport. Admission to the game, played in the evenings, is free. Many people come to watch and to place bets at the counters available. In Manila, many of the professional players are Basques from Spain. The sport is believed to have been invented by the Maya Indians of South America, and then introduced to Spain and its colonies by Spanish colonizers.

Filipinos are very keen on sports. They love to watch competitive team games as well as to take part in other popular activities such as chess, swimming, volleyball, tennis and horseracing. Sports provide the Filipinos with a much needed break from the routine of work.

Boys walking on stilts during a parade—another, less traditional, aspect of Filipino sporting activities which are very popular.

For about forty percent of the people of the Philippines, agriculture is the main source of income. The food crops grown are rice and maize. Maize is the staple food of most of the people of northern Mindanao and the Visayas. Enough of both crops are produced for the country's needs. Other food supplements include green vegetables, beans and root crops such as tapioca and sweet potatoes.

Life on the small, traditional rice farm is hard indeed. The farmer and his family do everything—from plowing and planting to harvesting and threshing the stalks of rice. Most of the work is done by hand, with only the *carabao* or water-buffalo to pull the plow. Progress is slow because of lack of funds for improvement, and lack of knowledge of modern agriculture methods.

In recent years, irrigation has been improved with the building of large dams on the island of Luzon. Experimental stations have been set up to develop new types of "miracle rice" that will produce better harvests. It is now possible to get three crops a year in the Central Plain to the north of Manila, even though traditional farming tools and methods still continue in use.

Cash crops include sugarcane, coconuts, Manila hemp, tobacco, and tropical fruits such as bananas and pineapples. Sugarcane is the most important cash crop. It has been grown in the Philippines for a very long time. Pineapples and bananas are two of the tropical fruits grown mainly on the island of Mindanao. They are among the chief export items of the Philippines today.

74

Ploughing rice paddies with a *carabao*.

Coconuts are the fruit of the tall and slender coconut palm. From the coconut comes coconut milk—a refreshing drink. The white flesh of the coconut can be eaten, or used for cooking or for making cakes. When dried, the flesh is known as copra from which oil can be extracted. This oil is used for cooking or for the manufacture of soap, perfume and lotions. The hard shell covering the coconut can be made into bowls or containers of many kinds. The coconut husk can be used as fuel or it can go into the making of door mats and twine. The ribs of the coconut leaves are made into brooms. Even the leaves and the trunk of the coconut palm are not wasted as they can be used for other household needs.

Sugarcane has long been farmed in the Philippines. The harvesting of the cane, shown here, is extremely arduous work.

Manila hemp, known also as *abaca*, comes from one variety of banana palm which does not produce edible fruit. It is used mainly in the making of strong ropes for shipping. Other uses include the making of mats, paper and fabrics. *Abaca* is grown in hot and wet areas—mainly in southeastern Luzon, the Visayan island of Samar and Leyte, and the island of Mindanao. One large *abaca*-growing area is near the city of Davao. Once the most well-known export from the Philippines, *abaca* has become less

76

important since synthetic materials such as rayon and nylon were made available in the world market.

Tobacco was introduced into the Philippines by the Spaniards in the sixteenth century. One variety grown today in northern Luzon is used for making the famous Philippine cigars. Another variety, grown on the islands of Panay, Negros and Cebu, is used in the local cigarette industry.

Most of the food and cash crops are grown on small farms, some of which are just over one acre (less than half a hectare) in size. On average, farms are between seven to ten acres (three and four hectares). There are very few large plantations in the Philippines. To feed the country's ever-increasing population, at least seventy percent of farming land in the Philippines is used to grow food crops. Cash crops take second place.

Land being cleared by the "slash and burn" method to make room for more crops. Most of the fertile land is used to grow food crops.

Fishing is another means of earning a living in the Philippines. It is done from small outrigger boats. Here again, traditional methods are used. The fish caught is enough for local consumption but not for export. Better boats and fishing equipment, refrigeration facilities and other improvements are needed before the Philippines can reap the rich harvests of the seas around the islands.

Timber used to be one of the main exports of the Philippines. The timber industry is well-developed with modern machinery being used to cut down trees and transport the logs. Unfortunately, the extensive export of timber in past years, the illegal cutting down of trees, the rapid growth of the population and the need to clear areas for farming, homes and industries have all greatly affected the country's resources. Stricter

This array of delicious seafood is characteristic of the Philippines. Not surprisingly, because of the surrounding seas, fish is widely eaten.

government supervision is now in force to make sure that forest areas are protected.

Copper is at the top of the list of minerals mined in the Philippines, mainly on the islands of Luzon and Mindanao. Other minerals include iron ore, chromium, manganese, coal, gold and silver. Oil is not found in large amounts but it is believed to be present in a number of areas. Although the Philippines is rich in mineral resources, mining development is slow. The main reason is the lack of funds. Mining operations can be very expensive.

Since the Philippines is largely an agricultural country, its industry is not as highly developed as that of some Asian countries. Most of the industries are concerned with either the manufacture of goods for the home market, or the processing of mineral and agricultural products for export. There are very few heavy industries.

Many small, cottage industries producing wood-carving and handicrafts such as baskets, hats, woven fabrics, embroidery and mats can be found in the rural areas. Other slightly larger enterprises producing shoes, bags, textiles, garments, furniture and food and drink items are found in the urban areas, especially in Metro Manila.

In recent years, more has been done to make use of the cheap, abundant labor available in the Philippines in industries producing goods for export. Other people work on products aimed at replacing goods imported from overseas. To the cigars, embroidery, baskets, hats and beer of past years are added

It is sandy quiet beaches like this one which help to attract tourists from other countries to the islands of the Philippines.

products such as electronic and electrical equipment, chemicals, aluminum pots and foils, glass, margarine, antibiotics and vitamins.

The trade of the Philippines has been mainly with the United States of America for more than fifty years. Japan is another important trading partner but the search for new markets in both Southeast Asia and Europe continues.

The building of hotels, offices and banks in Manila, the development of ports and industrial centers and the construction of roads and airports have all contributed to the improvement of the country. The main cities of the Philippines are now linked by

80

air services. There are also small inter-island ships or steamers for those who wish to travel by sea. Roads are served by buses, taxis and the colorful Filipino *jeepneys*. In certain towns, horse-drawn rigs or *calesas* still ply the roads as do the antique *tartanillas*—six-seater horse-drawn carriages. Travel up and down rivers can be done on river barges called *lorchas*. A narrow-gauge railroad also serves the island of Luzon.

Tourist arrivals are rapidly increasing. There were over one million foreign visitors in 1990 with the main attractions of the Philippines being the tropical setting of its many islands, the natural landscape, the fantastic shopping bargains and the bustling, cosmopolitan city of Manila.

6

Filipino Fiestas

Many festivals are celebrated in the Philippines every year, most of them of a religious nature. These celebrations or *fiestas*, as they are called in Spanish, are happy occasions. Almost everyone takes part in them.

As a people, Filipinos have a great capacity for enjoying the fun, laughter, color and drama of every *fiesta*. It is during such occasions that they demonstrate their fervent religious faith as well as their delight in being part of a crowd. Such enthusiastic and spiritual devotion go into these *fiestas* that they often become moving, joyous events whether they are celebrated throughout the nation or only in certain small towns and *barrios*.

In the Philippines, Christmas is the biggest celebration of all. It lasts for twenty-two days. Certainly the longest Yuletide celebration in the world, it starts on December 16th and lasts until the Feast of the Three Kings at the end of the first week in January.

At least two weeks before the Christmas season,

Iglesia ni Cristo (Christ's Church) in Manila.

schoolchildren busy themselves making bamboo cribs and barns. They carve wooden animals including the *carabao*, the Filipino farmer's ever-faithful friend. Other papier maché figures are made and all arranged to make up the well-known nativity scene depicting the birth of Jesus.

On the dawn of December 16th, church bells ring and Catholic masses are held in churches throughout the land. This continues for the next eight days. All over the Philippines, parts of the Christmas story are staged, with each region having its own variation of the traditional Christmas theme. Trees are trimmed, lights spring up everywhere and every garden and *plaza* is decorated with the nativity scene.

83

Festival floats—a typical feature of many Filipino fiestas.

On Christmas Eve, a midnight mass is held. Then comes a feast in the early hours of Christmas morning with family and friends giving each other gifts. In parts of the Visayas, Christmas Eve is celebrated with a huge bonfire in the town *plaza*.

In certain places, carolers dress as shepherds; in others, they sing and dance and perform comedy sketches. In the town of Kawit, south of Manila, Mary and Joseph's search for a room is dramatized.

New Year's Eve is celebrated with fireworks, parties and a lot of merrymaking. On New Year's Day, which is known as the

"Christmas of the Lovers" in the Philippines, sweethearts attend mass in church. They also exchange gifts. The Christmas season ends on January 6th.

The Philippines' most spectacular *fiesta* is Holy Week, the week before Easter Sunday. It is celebrated in either March or April. Holy Week tells of Christ's last seven days on earth. In Manila, thousands gather at Quiapo Church, in Manila's oldest district, on Palm Sunday. They wave braided palm fronds, and struggle to catch a drop or two of the holy water sprinkled on the crowd by the priests. Filipino Christians bring palm leaves to church to symbolize Christ's triumphant entry into Jerusalem. This event ushers in Holy Week in the Philippines.

From Holy Monday to Holy Friday, the Filipino version of the Passion Play is staged in towns and *barrios* throughout the land. During these plays, spectators sometimes leave talking, eating and drinking to join the actors on the stage. Often, the plays go off the subject of Christ to include other stories found in the Bible.

There are also processions throughout the week. In some places, penitents whip their bare backs as they walk through the streets. In some *barrios* in the provinces of Pampanga and Nueva Ecija on the Central Plain of Luzon, actual crucifixions take place at noon on Good Friday. Some devout Filipinos take on the role of the cross-bearing Christ. They are then nailed to the cross and left to bleed for a short while. In other parts of the country, other Filipino Christians spend Good Friday meditating on Christ's death.

Holy Saturday is a calm and quiet day. At midnight, prayers begin. Churches are in total darkness at the start of the service. This is to remind the faithful of the darkness of sin into which mankind was plunged when Christ died on the Cross. Then, at a particular moment during the Mass, candles are lit, church bells rung, organ music played and sacred images unveiled. Christ has risen and the earth is once more filled with light.

On the following day, which is Easter Sunday, church bells ring joyfully to announce the good news of Christ's resurrection. There is much rejoicing and celebration.

The Holy Week *fiesta* celebrated on the island of Marinduque is even more fantastic. Known as the Moriones Festival, it is celebrated mainly in the capital city of Boac and the towns of Gasan and Mogpog.

Marinduque is a small, volcanic island lying between Mindoro Island (due south of Manila) and the Bondoc peninsula in southern Luzon. This heart-shaped island has a beautiful legend attached to it. A long, long time ago, Marin, the daughter of a southern Luzon king, fell in love with a poet-fisherman named Garduke. Their forbidden love, resulting in the order for Garduke's execution, made the young lovers sail out to sea where they drowned themselves. There and then, an island arose out of the waters. It was named *Marin-duque*.

During the Moriones Festival which begins on Holy Wednesday, the townsfolk of Boac, Gasan and Mogpog in Marinduque dress up as Roman centurions or *Morions*, complete with Roman-style plumed helmets. They roam the streets of their

86

Marinduque islanders dressed up for the Moriones festival, which is essentially a re-enactment of the crucifixion of Christ.

towns wearing carved wooden masks with angry expressions painted on them. There are parades each day with local bands playing music ranging from hymns to jazz.

The main event starts with a re-enactment of the crucifixion of Christ on Good Friday. The story of the Roman centurion, Longinus, is also relived all over again. Longinus was blind in one eye. He was the Roman soldier who pierced Christ's left side with a lance so that Christ could die without prolonged suffering. The story tells how Longinus could see again when a drop of Christ's blood flew into his blind eye. The centurion became a

87

Christian when he witnessed Christ's resurrection while guarding the tomb. The Roman authorities sent soldiers to pursue him when he started preaching the gospel. He was arrested, brought to trial and beheaded.

The story of Longinus is dramatized in Marinduque on Sunday. Christ has risen and the exciting chase of Longinus begins. Twice he escapes from the *Morions* as he flees, but eventually he is caught, tried and executed. His supposedly headless body (without the carved mask and helmet) is carried aloft on a bamboo pallet to the church. One of the most colorful festivals in the Philippines, the Moriones Festival in Marinduque attracts not only fellow Filipinos from the other islands but tourists also.

Another festival that rivals it in color and drama is the Ati-Atihan. This *fiesta* is celebrated mainly in the town of Kalibo on the island of Panay in the Visayas. It is usually held during the third week of January.

Actually a pre-Christian festival, the original Ati-Atihan was held to celebrate the friendship agreement between the *Negritos* (*Atis* or *Aeta*) and some Malay *datus* or chiefs who came to settle on Panay Island during the thirteenth century. The Malay *datus* who had fled from their homes in Borneo, bought some land from the *Negritos*. At a feast in honor of their new friends, the grateful *datus* good-humoredly blackened themselves with soot to receive their dark-skinned guests.

About four or five centuries later, the people of Panay became Christians. According to an often-told tale, the islanders were

An impressive headdress worn for the festival of Ati-Athan.

once attacked by the Muslim pirates of Mindanao. However, the sudden appearance of the *Santo Nino*—the Christ Child—frightened off the raiders.

Today, the Ati-Atihan in the Philippines combines three celebrations into one—the celebration of friendship between the *Negritos* and the Malay *datus*, the feast of the island's patron saint, Santo Nino, and the island's harvest thanksgiving.

89

The *fiesta* lasts for three days. During this time, the happy islanders cover themselves with soot from head to toe. Then, dressed as fierce but colorful thirteenth-century Ati warriors, they sing, drink, dance and take part in noisy street parades. Nowadays, some participants even dress as astronauts or Walt Disney characters.

On Sunday, the last day of the Ati-Atihan celebrations, there is a Mass in the Church of the Santo Nino. For the sick, the image of the *Santo Nino*—believed to have healing powers—is rubbed over arms, legs and backs. Finally, a four-hour procession with decorated floats takes to the streets. Women, singing hymns and saying their rosaries, join in the parade together with all the other jubilant participants.

Yet another interesting festival in the Philippines is the Feast of the Black Nazarene. Every year, on January 9th, male devotees carry a life-size statue of Christ bearing the cross, out of the old Quiapo Church in Manila. The statue, stained a dark brown by the unknown Mexican convert who carved it about four centuries ago, was brought to Manila from Mexico during the early days of the Spanish conquest.

The statue of the Black Nazarene, with its crown of thorns and an expression of suffering on its face, is paraded through the streets, followed by the image of the Virgin Mary. The procession starts in the afternoon and goes on until twilight when candles are lit. Everyone in the streets tries to touch the Black Nazarene with either a towel or a handkerchief, for the statue is believed to have miraculous powers. These pieces of cloth are then rubbed onto the body to cleanse it of sins or illness. At the end of the day, the Black Nazarene is returned to its shrine in Quiapo Church.

In the festivals celebrated in the Philippines, the farmer's faithful friend, the *carabao*, is not forgotten. In mid-May, during summer, the Carabao Festival is celebrated in Pulilan and a few other towns in the Central Plain of Luzon. The festival is held in honor of San Isidro Labrador, the patron saint and protector of the farmers. The *carabao*, of course, plays an important part in the celebration.

At dawn, each farmer cleans, scrubs and decorates his *carabao*. It is then hitched to the family cart which is beautifully decorated with flowers, leaves and bunting. The family, dressed in its best, gets into the cart which is loaded with fruits, farming tools and an image of San Isidro Labrador.

The procession of carts then heads for the church, together with village bands in their trucks, and gaily decorated floats depicting farming life. The local beauty queen is always part of such parades.

On reaching the church, each *carabao* is unhitched to join the *carabao* parade which is led past the church. The *carabao* are made to kneel in front of the church, and a priest blesses the farm animals. Later, there are *carabao* races in the center of the town, as well as other contests and games.

Elsewhere in the Philippines, during the summer and at other times of the year, various harvest festivals, flower parades, water processions and *fiestas* in honor of patron saints are held.

91

A farmer with his *carabao* which will draw the decorated family cart to take part in the Carabao Festival.

There are also non-Christian festivals—those celebrated in the Muslim south and those celebrated by the animist mountain tribes of northern Luzon and various other minority groups. Tribal festivals include harvest celebrations, rain dances and planting rites.

Muslim festivals include the birthday of the Prophet Muhammad, *Hari Raya Hadji* which celebrates the end of the yearly holy pilgrimage to Mecca in Saudi Arabia, and *Hari Raya Paosa* which celebrates the end of the month of fasting.

Then, for all Filipinos, there are the celebrations of Independence Day on June 12th, the Filipino-American

Friendship Day on July 4th, not to mention Bataan Day which commemorates the fall of Bataan to the Japanese and the "Death March" of many Filipino and American soldiers.

Festivals in the Philippines are indeed unique occasions. Once seen they are not easily forgotten.

7

The Philippines Today

The Philippines has always been a difficult country to govern. Since early times its scattered islands, difficult communications, religious divisions and cultural differences have made it hard for the people to think of themselves as a single nation. Conditions were such that it was easier for the people to remain loyal to their own family, community and racial group than to the country as a whole.

A rapidly-growing population and an ever-widening gap between the rich and the poor in modern times have also not made things easier. One of the country's greatest needs was to grow enough food for the people. Another was to have money to improve and support agricultural growth, to develop the country and to promote trade and industry.

In the Philippines today, businessmen and those in the various professions make up only a small group of people living mainly in the cities. Another group consists of rich families who own large areas of land. The rest of the people—believed to be almost

94

three-quarters of the population—live in poverty. The unemployed poor in the city slums are even worse off than the poor tenant farmers in the countryside.

The poor have no spending power. They have no money to buy goods or products manufactured in local factories. This, in turn, makes it difficult for the nation's newly-developed industries to grow, expand and sell their goods more cheaply. Without the necessary growth and expansion, it becomes impossible for more people to be employed. The situation becomes even more problematic as the birth rate continues to rise.

The crime rate in the Philippines is high; maintaining law and

A young woman who has no spending power and no modern kitchen—but what she has she keeps neat and clean.

order is one of the government's major problems. Many people carry arms, and killings occur quite often during election time. There is also the armed threat from the Muslims (Moro National Liberation Front, or MNLF) and the communists (New People's Army, or NPA).

The Muslims from the southern provinces of the Sulu Islands, Mindanao and Palawan want to break away from the rest of the Philippines to form a separate state. The Communists, who operate on most of the major islands of the Philippines, are also a force that cannot be ignored. In 1996, their number was estimated to include some 120,000 guerrillas, half of whom were believed to be armed. The reasons why people in the countryside join the Communists can be traced mainly to poverty, discontent and the brutality of an often corrupt and undisciplined military force.

The Philippines did, in the 1970s, see an improvement in law and order. Major roads and dams were built, the nation became self-sufficient in rice and there was economic growth. Unfortunately, not all policies were successfully implemented. Land reform, which was introduced to ensure that more farmers owned the rented land they tilled, met with resistance from rich, landowning families who had great political power.

Several wealthy families were deprived of their power, and some social changes were made. But, in time, new favored families took their place, especially in the areas of commerce and industry. Corruption, never totally destroyed, continued. So did the gap between the rich and the poor, bringing with it social

The Pantabangan Dam on Luzon, built during the 1970s.

discontent and bitter disappointment in Marcos' twenty-year rule, nine years of which (from 1972 to 1981) were under martial law.

Many other problems continued to make the task of ruling the Philippines an extremely difficult one. In the early 1980s, the energy crisis, world-wide recession and the drop in the prices of sugar, copper, coconuts and other important exports of the Philippines led to a slump in the country's economy.

The Philippines, badly in need of funds, had to borrow heavily from outside, thus increasing its foreign debt. The fall in value of the country's currency, the *peso*, did not help. Neither did the growing disillusion with the Marcos government.

In 1983, the assassination of the opposition leader, Benigno Aquino, as he returned from the United States, led to further unrest. Finally, in early 1986, the country went to the polls. Controversial election results led the Filipino people to turn against Marcos. Filipinos took to the streets of Manila in support of the opposition candidate, Corazon Aquino, widow of Benigno Aquino. This revolution, carried out without much bloodshed, resulted in Marcos leaving the Philippines, and Corazon Aquino being sworn in as the new President of the Philippines on February 25, 1986.

It was a critical time for the Philippines, faced as it was with near economic and political ruin. Fortunately for the country, the support of the people, the Church and the military for Aquino's takeover resulted in more confidence in business. The Philippines

Foresters at work. Timber is one of the Philippines' most valuable resources.

had also been given more time to repay its loans and was successful in getting more aid, especially from the United States, to boost its ailing economy.

One of President Aquino's immediate tasks was to appoint her Cabinet. Another was to try to resolve the Communist and Muslim rebellion in the country by peaceful means if possible. Yet another urgent task was to make the country's military force a more professional organization.

In 1992, Fidel V. Ramos was elected president with less than 24 percent of the overall vote. The government's 1996 treaty with the Moro National Liberation Front (MNLF) failed to bring peace to the southern islands. Economic problems hit the Philippines in 1997, with a drought that affected half of the country's rice crops.

There are many more important jobs to be done before the Philippines can be transformed into a stable, developing nation. Many problems remain difficult to solve. But the land and its people are not without potential.

Although poor, the Philippines is agriculturally fertile. It is also blessed with resources such as copper, gold, cement and sulphur from the earth, timber from the forests and fish, pearls and shells from the surrounding seas. The natural beauty of its sunny, tropical islands and its warm, friendly people are all valuable assets.

Today, with a government and President determined not only to cut down on waste, corruption and violence, but also to woo investors to help build the country, it is hoped that the Filipino people will unite and persevere in finding the best way of ruling their beautiful but complex island home.

GLOSSARY

abaca	Manila hemp produced from a variety of banana palm
animism	Belief that animals and things have souls; and that the world is full of spirits
archipelago	An expanse of water with many scattered islands
barrio	Village
carabao	Water buffalo that pulls the plow on many farms
Christians	Believers in the teachings of Jesus, believed to be the Son of God
fault zone	An area that is very prone to earthquakes
haribon	A monkey-eating eagle found only in some of the mountain ranges of the Philippines. With a wing-span of almost six feet it is the largest eagle in the world.
jeepneys	Public transportation vehicles that are decorated very colorfully. Originally old army jeeps remade to carry ten passengers, they are now manufactured in the Philippines specifically for public transportation
maize	Indian corn

mestizo	People of a racial mix of Indian and Spanish
Mindanao Trench	A trench on the ocean floor to the east of Mindanao Island six times deeper then the Grand Canyon. The second deepest spot on the ocean floor.
Muslims	Followers of the Islamic religion which follows the teachings of the Prophet Muhammad
Tagalog	Philippines national language
tarsier	A small monkey with a head and body measuring only six inches. It has a long tail and large eyes and can make a 180-degree turn with its head. It is found only on islands of volcanic origin.
terno	A long dress with puff sleeves that is the female national costume
turo-turo	Philippine modern version of a fast-food eating place
typhoon	Tropical storm with strong winds and heavy rainfall (*bagyos*)

INDEX